DISCOVER MAPS WITH ORDNANCE SURVEY

Patricia Harrison
Steve Harrison

Contents

This is a picture of a group of children at Revoe School. They are busy working. We can see what some of the children are doing but we cannot see what Shirin and Joanne are doing.

WHAT IS A MAP?

We can see what everyone is doing if we look down at the table from above. This is called a plan view. Plan means the same as map.

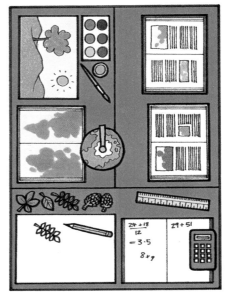

▶ Who is Adam next to? Who is he opposite?

▶ Now write who is next to and opposite Bobby, Suey and Charlie.

▶ Did you look at the picture or the plan for your answer?

▶ Charlie is painting a picture. Write a sentence to say what each child is doing.

▶ Did you look at the picture or the plan for your answer?

▶ How many children have a chair in the classroom?

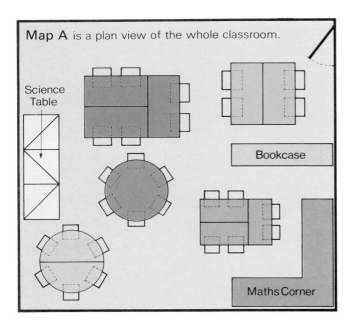

Map A is a plan view of the whole classroom.

Science Table

Bookcase

Maths Corner

▶ Is the bookcase or the maths corner nearer to the door?

▶ Which shapes can you see on the classroom plan?

▶ Draw a plan of a table top.

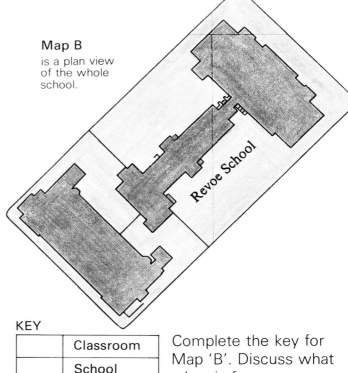

Map B is a plan view of the whole school.

Revoe School

KEY

	Classroom
	School
	Playground

Complete the key for Map 'B'. Discuss what a key is for.

▶ Now draw a key for Map 'A'.

The *Ordnance Survey* make maps. They use photographs taken from aeroplanes to draw accurate maps. This is an *aerial photograph* of Revoe School and the streets around it.

You can see many details clearly on the map and on the photograph but some details are only shown on the map or the photograph.

Copy and complete this chart. Tick the box if the detail can be seen on the map, photo or both. One has been done for you.

details	aerial photo	map c
house numbers		
chimney pots		
road names		
houses	✓	✓
cars		
methodist Church		
bowling green		

▶ Which sports can be played in the area?
▶ What was the weather like on the day the photo was taken?
▶ Why is this important?

This map shows the same area as the aerial photograph.

Map C

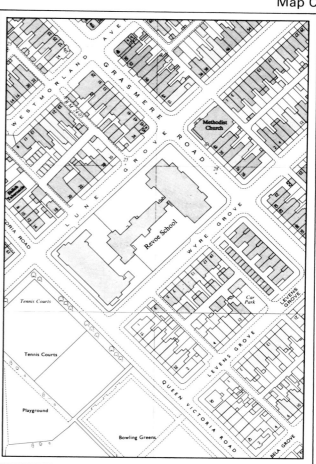

▶ Match each drawing with the correct plan view.

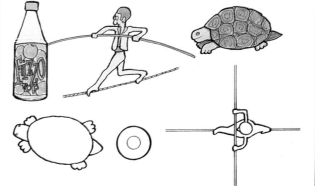

Using Local Maps

Find out as much as you can about your local area by using an Ordnance Survey Map.

Try to find your home and your friends' homes. What sports are available?

Are there any short cuts you didn't know about?

INVESTIGATING A CHURCH

A church can be great fun to visit when you know what to look for. You may be surprised at how much you can learn about a church before you even visit. Use this map to help you write the correct ending for each sentence.

▶ **The church is**
(a) near the river
(b) a long way from the river

▶ **The church is**
(a) Roman Catholic
(b) Church of England

▶ **St. Wilfred's is**
(a) in the centre of the village
(b) at the edge of the village

▶ **The Rector (Vicar) lives**
(a) close to the church
(b) far from the church

▶ **Long ago the area was used for**
(a) a Roman fort
(b) a Norman castle

▶ **The church is**
(a) west of the river
(b) east of the river

▶ **The river is**
(a) west of the church
(b) east of the church

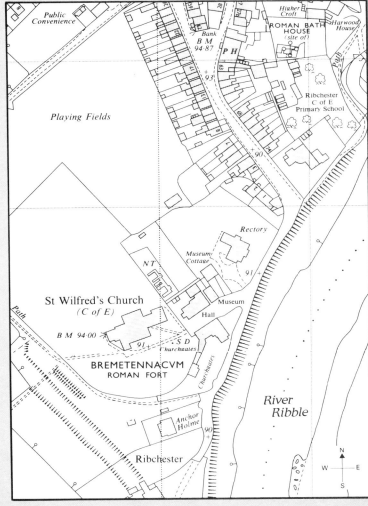

KEY

N.T. National Trust
S.D. Sun Dial
P.H. Public House
------- Footpath
Slope. Thin end points down.

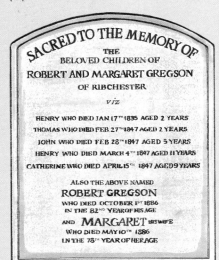

SACRED TO THE MEMORY OF
THE
BELOVED CHILDREN OF
ROBERT AND MARGARET GREGSON
OF RIBCHESTER

viz

HENRY WHO DIED JAN 17TH 1835 AGED 2 YEARS
THOMAS WHO DIED FEB 27TH 1847 AGED 2 YEARS
JOHN WHO DIED FEB 28TH 1847 AGED 5 YEARS
HENRY WHO DIED MARCH 4TH 1847 AGED 11 YEARS
CATHERINE WHO DIED APRIL 15TH 1847 AGED 9 YEARS

ALSO THE ABOVE NAMED
ROBERT GREGSON
WHO DIED OCTOBER 1ST 1886
IN THE 82ND YEAR OF HIS AGE
AND MARGARET HIS WIFE
WHO DIED MAY 10TH 1886
IN THE 78TH YEAR OF HER AGE

This is a picture of a gravestone in St. Wilfred's churchyard.
▶ How many children did Robert and Margaret Gregson have?
▶ How old was John when he died?
▶ When did Thomas die?
▶ How many daughters did they have?
▶ How many of their children died in 1847?

▶ How old were Robert and Margaret Gregson when they died?
▶ Did Robert or Margaret die first?
▶ Why do you think two of their children were called Henry?
▶ What could have been the cause of so many children dying in 1847?
▶ How could we find out what the children died of?

Name of church		
Draw the three different arch shapes and label them		
What materials are used for		
Doors	Walls	Roof
Choose the correct symbol for this church		

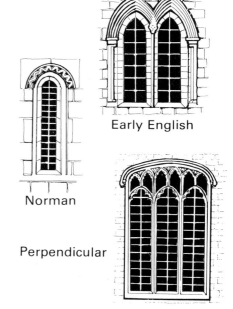

Early English

Norman

Perpendicular

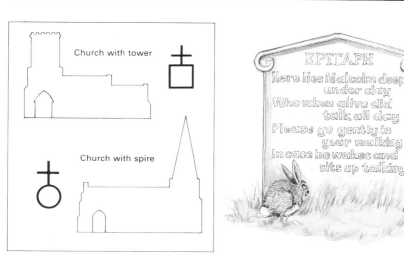

Church with tower

Church with spire

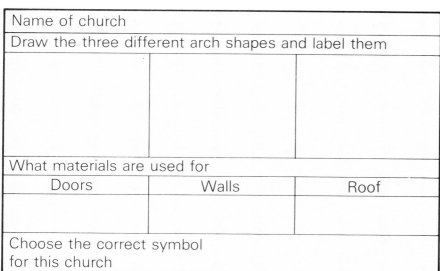

EPITAPH

Here lies Malcolm deep under clay
Who when alive did talk all day
Please go gently in your walking
In case he wakes and sits up talking

Write epitaphs for yourself and a friend.

Using Local Maps

Choose a church in your local area.
Use local maps to discover as much as you can about the church before you make a visit.

5

The farmer swerved to avoid a cat. Seconds later he crashed and the side of his lorry was smashed. Out raced his bull and THEN the trouble began.

BULLY GOES TO TOWN

The map on the opposite page shows the eight places visited by Bully.

▶ Describe what is happening in each picture.

▶ Choose one of the pictures and write a report for the local newspaper. Think about the headline, details and what happened next.

▶ Match the picture with a location on the map. Do it like this — 'Bully went into the Bull and Royal Hotel which is next to the Parish Church on Church St.'

Bully caused so much trouble the police were called.

Here are the messages car 16 received. Follow car 16's route on the map and say where it stops each time.

▶ Turn right out of the Police Station into Earl St., left along Lancaster Rd., right at Old Vicarage. Stop on the left just after Bishopgate.

Where are you?

▶ Continue to Tithebarn St. and turn right. Stop on the right where a canopy covers the pavement.

Where are you?

▶ Go along Tithebarn St., pass Crooked Lane and turn right into Lord St. Turn left at Lancaster Rd., then first right. Stop on the left between the bus shelters.

Where are you?

▶ Continue along Harris St., turn left into Birley St. and carry on past Jacson St. to Fishergate. Turn left and drive on past Lancaster Rd. and the bank. Stop on the left at the third building after Tithebarn St.

Where are you?

▶ Drive back along Church St. passing the church on your left. Stop at the hotel opposite the Red Lion.

Where are you?

▶ Return along Church St. Turn left into Tithebarn St. Stop on the left after the Empire Hotel.

Where are you?

▶ Go along Tithebarn St. Stop at the building on the right which faces Crooked Lane.

Where are you?

▶ Give directions for car 16 to continue to — a) the Police Station b) the Town Hall   c) the baths.

▶ Draw a picture and write about what Bully did at each of these three places.

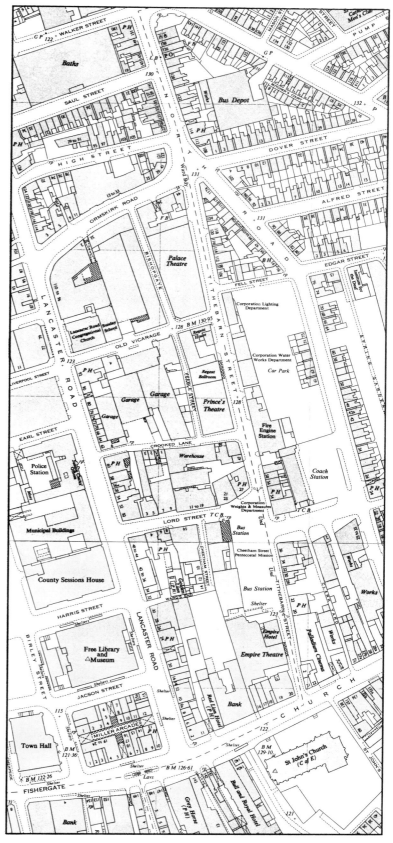

Using Local Maps

What could Bully do in your local area?

Use a 1:2500 map of your locality and describe Bully's routes to a partner.

Sissy Norton and her dad are touring Scotland. They are travelling by motor bike. Sissy is in charge of checking routes and distances.

SCOTLAND HERE WE COME

▶ 1. Which roads will Sissy choose to travel along?
The first one is done for you.
(a) From Fort William to Inverness — *travel along the A82.*
(b) From Ayr to Glasgow.
(c) From Glasgow to Stranraer.
(d) From Dundee to Aberdeen.
(e) From Oban to Fort William.

▶ 2. Which towns will they pass through on these journeys?
(a) From Aberdeen to Braemar along the A93.
(b) From Ayr to Stranraer along the A77.
(c) From John O' Groats to Inverness along the A9.
(d) From Glasgow to Fort William along the A82
(e) From Aberdeen to Dundee along the A92.

Sissy and her dad planned their route for the week.
Here is Sissy's diary.
Can you complete it for her by using the map?

Monday
Start from Berwick on Tweed travel north along the A_____ through D_____. Next stop the city of E_____.

Tuesday
Cross the F_____ Bridge to D_____, travel north to Perth along the M__.

Wednesday
Leave Perth early, travel along the A_____ to Dundee and eat cakes for lunch.
Drive to Aberdeen along the A92 passing through A_____, M_____, I_____ and S_____.

Thursday
Today we will drive to John o'Groats. It will be a long journey We'll travel along the A_____ to Inverness. After lunch we'll take the A9 north passing through Allness, T_____ to B_____ Bridge, on to D_____, north to G_____ and on to H_____. The last town before John o'Groats is W_____.

▶ 3. Sissy and her dad will finish their holiday at Fort William on Saturday. Complete Sissy's diary.

Aberdeen												
177	Ayr											
182	134	Berwick on Tweed										
59	143	148	Braemar									
67	117	113	52	Dundee								
125	73	57	91	56	Edinburgh							
165	133	190	125	127	144	Fort William						
145	33	101	110	83	44	101	Glasgow					
105	199	215	75	132	158	66	166	Inverness				
232	328	342	202	259	285	195	295	129	John O' Groats			
189	212	552	159	186	216	79	179	84	189	Kyle of Lochalsh		
178	125	180	141	117	123	49	92	115	244	128	Oban	
228	51	158	194	167	124	184	84	250	379	263	176	Stranraer

In miles

How to Use this Mileage Chart
Point to Glasgow with your right hand. Point to Aberdeen with your left hand. Move your right hand across and your left hand down. They meet at 145 miles. The distance from Aberdeen to Glasgow is 145 miles.

▶ 1. Using the mileage chart. How far is it from
(a) Dundee to Oban?
(b) Inverness to Ayr?
(c) Stranraer to Fort William?

▶ 2. If Sissy and her dad visit the following places how many miles will they travel altogether?
Stranraer to Edinburgh
Edinburgh to Dundee
Dundee to Glasgow

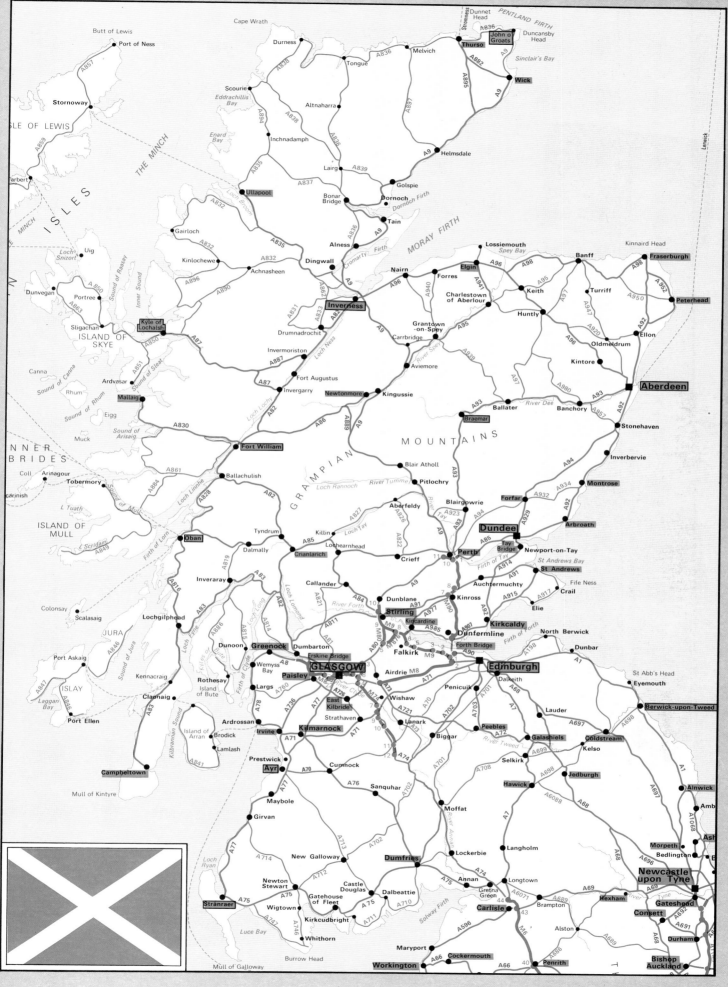

ISLE OF LEWIS
Butt of Lewis
Port of Ness
Stornoway
Harbert
THE MINCH
OUTER ISLES
A857
A859

Cape Wrath
Durness
A838
Scourie
Eddrachillis Bay
Enard Bay
Inchnadamph
A894
A838
Ullapool
A835
A832
A833
A837
Lairg
A839
Bonar Bridge
A836
A9

Dunnet Head
Stromness
PENTLAND FIRTH
Thurso
John o' Groats
Duncansby Head
A836
A882
Wick
A895
A9
Sinclair's Bay

Melvich
Tongue
A836
Altnaharra
A836
A897

Helmsdale
A9
Golspie
Dornoch
Dornoch Firth
Tain
A9
Alness
Cromarty Firth
Dingwall

Gairloch
A832
Kinlochewe
Achnasheen
A896
A890
A832
A835
A862
A9
Inverness

Loch Snizort
Uig
Dunvegan
A850
Portree
A863
Sligachan
ISLAND OF SKYE
A851
A87
Kyle of Lochalsh
A850
A890
Drumnadrochit
Loch Ness
A887
Invermoriston
Fort Augustus
A87
Invergarry

MORAY FIRTH
Nairn
A96
Forres
Elgin
Lossiemouth
Spey Bay
Banff
A96
A98
Kinnaird Head
Fraserburgh
A98
A952
Peterhead
A950
A92
Ellon
A920
Oldmeldrum
Kintore
A96
A93
Aberdeen

A940
A941
Charlestown of Aberlour
Keith
A95
Huntly
A97
Turriff
A947
A96
A980

Grantown-on-Spey
Carrbridge
A95
Aviemore
River Spey
A939
A93
A97

Canna
Rhum
Eigg
Muck
Sound of Canna
Sound of Rhum
INNER HEBRIDES
Coll
Arinagour
carinish

Ardvasar
Sound of Sleat
Mallaig
A830
A861
A884
Tobermory
ISLAND OF MULL
L Scridain
A849

Newtonmore
Kingussie
A86
A889
A9
Braemar
A93
Ballater
GRAMPIAN MOUNTAINS
River Dee
Banchory
A93
A957
Stonehaven
Inverbervie
A94
A92

Blair Atholl
Loch Rannoch
River Tummel
Pitlochry
A924
Aberfeldy
A827
A826
Blairgowrie
A923
A93
Forfar
A932
A934
Montrose
A92
A929
Arbroath
A94

Fort William
Ballachulish
A82
A828
Loch Linnhe
Firth of Lorn
Oban
A85
A816
Dalmally
Crianlarich
A85
Tyndrum
Killin
Loch Tay
Lochearnhead
A822
Crieff
A85
River Tay
Perth
11
10
Dundee
Tay Bridge
Newport-on-Tay
St Andrews Bay
St Andrews
Fife Ness
Crail

Inveraray
A819
A83
Callander
A821
River Forth
Dunblane
A91
Stirling
A84
10
A9
8
7
Kinross
A977
M90
Auchtermuchty
A914
A91
A915
A917
Elie
A823

Lochgilphead
A816
A83
A886
Loch Fyne
Loch Long
A814
A811
M80
M9
Kincardine
A985
Dunfermline
A907
Kirkcaldy
Firth of Forth
North Berwick
A198
Dunbar
A1
St Abb's Head
Eyemouth
Berwick-upon-Tweed

Dunoon
Greenock
Dumbarton
Erskine Bridge
Wemyss Bay
Paisley
GLASGOW
A8
Falkirk
M9
Forth Bridge
A90
Edinburgh
A71
Penicuik
Dalkeith
A68
A703
A701
A7
Lauder
A697
A698

Colonsay
Scalasaig
JURA
Port Askaig
A846
Kennacraig
Kyles of Bute
Rothesay
Island of Bute
Largs
A760
Claonaig
ISLAY
Port Ellen
Laggan Bay
A847
A846

Airdrie
M8
Wishaw
A721
A70
A702
A72
Peebles
Biggar
A701
River Tweed
Galashiels
Coldstream
Kelso
A699
Selkirk
A708
Jedburgh
A698
Hawick
A6088
A68

Ardrossan
Irvine
A78
A736
Kilmarnock
A71
A77
East Kilbride
Strathaven
Lanark
A73
7
9
10
11
12
A74
A71
Brodick
Lamlash
Island of Arran

Prestwick
Ayr
A70
A77
Cumnock
A76
Maybole
Girvan
A714
A713
Sanquhar
A702
Moffat
A7
Lockerbie
Langholm
A7

Campbeltown
Mull of Kintyre
A83

New Galloway
Loch Ryan
Newton Stewart
A75
A712
Gatehouse of Fleet
A75
Castle Douglas
Dalbeattie
A710
Kirkcudbright
A711
Whithorn
Wigtown
A746
A747
Luce Bay
Burrow Head
Mull of Galloway

Dumfries
A75
Annan
A74
Gretna Green
Longtown
A6071
Carlisle
44
43
Brampton
A689
Alston
A686

Stranraer
A75

Maryport
A66
Cockermouth
Workington
A66
A596
40
Penrith
M6

Newcastle upon Tyne
Gateshead
Consett
A691
Durham
Bishop Auckland
A68
A689
Alnwick
Amb
Ash
Morpeth
Bedlington
A1068
A697
A1
A696
Hexham
A69
River Tyne
Lenwick

Every year many people visit Aviemore for their holidays. Aviemore is popular in summer and in winter.

AVIEMORE

A

B

C

J

These photographs show some of the activities people can enjoy at different times of the year.

▶ Copy and complete the chart to show when activities take place.

PHOTO	ACTIVITY	WINTER	SUMMER	ALL YEAR
A	Disco			✔
B				
C				

▶ Say which of the activities shown here will be most popular with (a) children, (b) adults, or (c) both.

▶ List the activities putting your favourite first.
▶ Now make a list for your grandmother.

▶ Choose four activities and describe what you would wear for them. Then say why the clothes you choose are sensible.

▶ Look at this list of other activities at Aviemore.
Cinema, tennis, steam railway, swimming.
Draw a picture and write a sentence about each one.

I

H

D

F

E

G

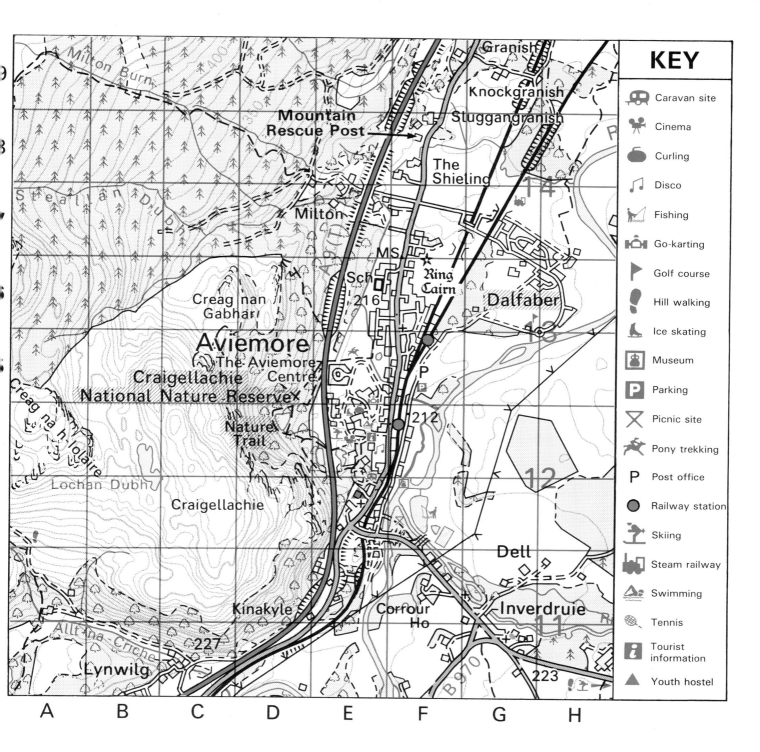

KEY

🚐	Caravan site
🎥	Cinema
🥌	Curling
🎵	Disco
🎣	Fishing
🏎️	Go-karting
⛳	Golf course
👣	Hill walking
⛸️	Ice skating
🏛️	Museum
P	Parking
✕	Picnic site
🐎	Pony trekking
P	Post office
●	Railway station
🎿	Skiing
🚂	Steam railway
〰️	Swimming
🎾	Tennis
🛈	Tourist information
▲	Youth hostel

▶ In which grid square would you find the following activities?
The first one has been done for you.

Activity	Grid Square
Tennis	G1

Nature trail; car parking; skating; go karts; pony trekking; swimming; disco; cinema.

▶ Now list the grid squares for your six favourite activities.

▶ Plan a day in Aviemore for

(a) A sunny winter's day
(b) A rainy winter's day
(c) A wet summer's day
(d) A hot summer's day

▶ Can you discover what is a National Nature Reserve?
What animals might you find there?
Is there a nature reserve near where you live?

11

THEN AND NOW

O.S. Maps show us what our local area looks like now. Older O.S. Maps show us what the same area used to look like.

These two maps show Birmingham City Centre. One map is modern, the other is from 1890. Look carefully at the two maps and you will see what has changed and what has stayed the same.

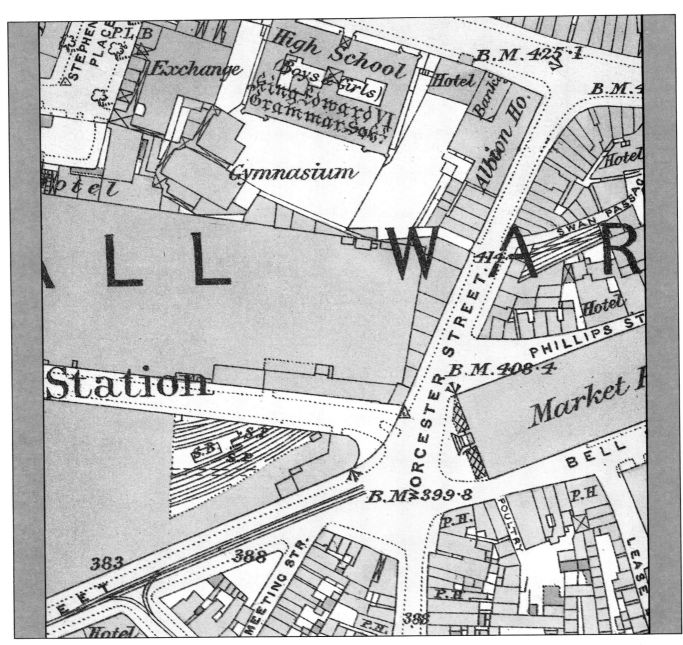

▶ Look at the two maps and list the streets that appear —

(a) Only on the 1890 map.

(b) Only on the modern map.

▶ Which road names give clues to the buildings that might be found in them?

▶ Read the list of activities. Copy and complete the chart to show which can be done now and which were done in 1890. Two have been done for you.

1. Watch a film
2. Buy fruit in the Market Hall
3. Undercover shopping
4. Go to the Grammar School
5. Walk under the road
6. Stay in a hotel
7. Live in Old Meeting St.
8. Catch a steam train
9. Catch a bus

Then	Now
Buy fruit in the market hall	Watch a film

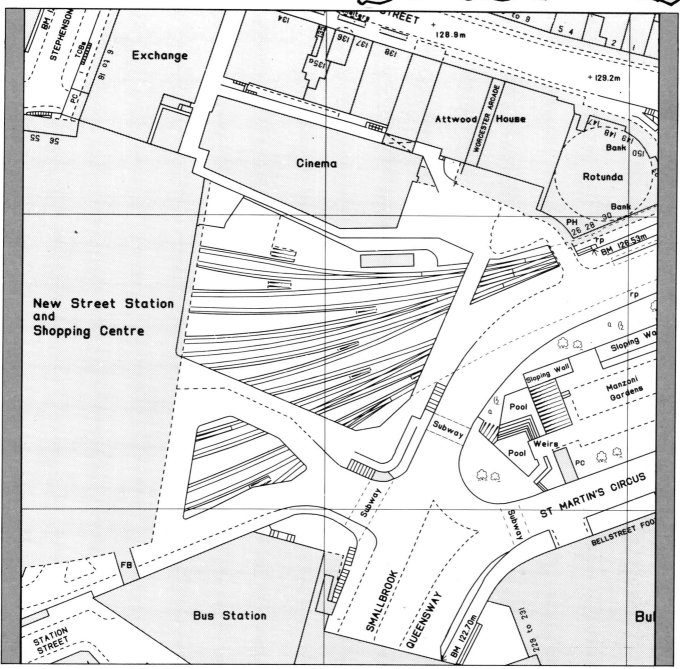

13

Rip Van Winkle was given a strange potion to drink back in 1890. He fell into a deep sleep and has just woken up. As he climbed out of the sewer system he could not believe his eyes — Birmingham had changed so much!

100 YEARS ON

what time is it?

▶ Look at the eight pictures around Rip. Four of the pictures show what he expected to find, the other four show what he did find. Copy and complete the chart.

PICTURE	EXPECTED	FOUND
A	Steam Train	Electric Train
B		
C		
D		

▶ Now draw what he would find instead of pictures E-H.

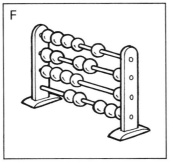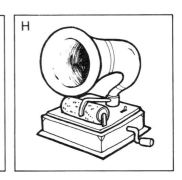

Rip decided to visit some of the places he remembered. Look back at the two maps.

▶ What did he find when he reached the gymnasium site?

▶ What did he find when he reached the school site?

MANZONI GARDENS

BUS STATION

▶ What had he expected to find at the site of the pool?

▶ Which street did he expect to be in when he stood in the bus station?

Imagine *you* have been asleep for 100 years.
What would be strange in your local area?
Write a story about the day you woke up and what happened to you. Describe your feelings.

When you arrive home tonight you will find a strange machine in your bedroom — a time machine. Sit in the cockpit, press the button marked 2090 and within seconds you will be in the next century.

▶ Describe your adventures. Draw a picture of your local area in 100 years time. Draw a simple map to show what changes you think will take place.

Using Local Maps

You can find out the changes in your own area or town by looking at local maps. Compare a modern map of your area with one from the past. Talk to older people. Ask them if they remember the area as it used to be. Do they know *when* the changes happened?

MY NAME IS ADAM BAKER. BAKER IS A CLUE ABOUT MY FAMILY LONG AGO.

CLUES TO THE PAST

Surnames give clues to our family history.
Place names give clues to our country's history.

MY NAME IS YASMIN PATEL. PATEL IS A CLUE ABOUT MY FAMILY LONG AGO.

Place names on a map tell us about the people who once lived there. When Celtic people settled in an area they gave the place a Celtic name. Saxon settlers used their own words to name places. The Viking people brought Viking names with them when they came to Britain.

		Word	Meaning
Celtic		pen	hill or high place
		tre or trev	hamlet (small village)
Saxon		ham	hamlet
		ton	village
		ley	field
		field	field
		ing	family or people
Viking		by	village
		thorpe	hamlet

▶ Look carefully at the three maps. Use the chart to help you decide which of the maps shows a Celtic area. Write down all the Celtic names you can see. Do the same for the Saxon and Viking areas.

A

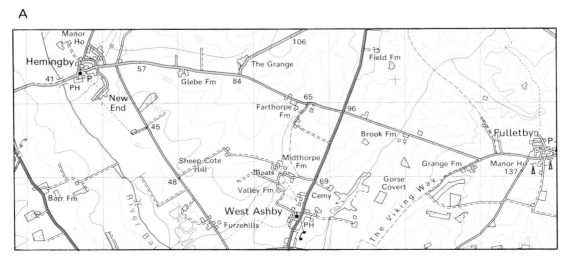

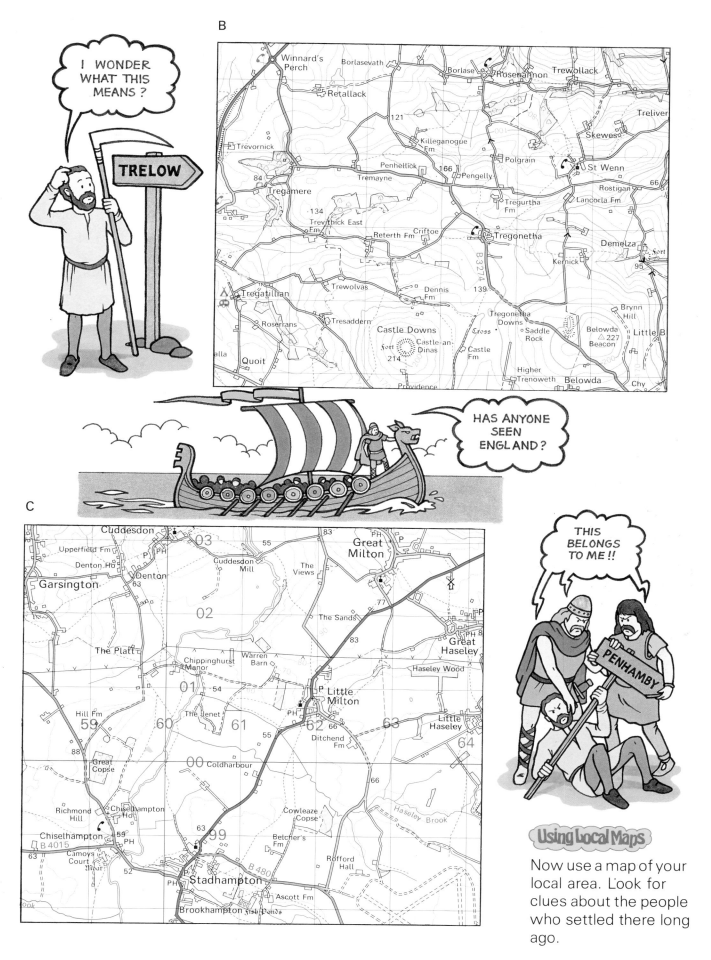

Six pupils from the local school visited Brookhouse Farm to carry out a *farm survey*. They used a 1:2500 Ordnance Survey Map. They visited the fields and farmyard and recorded the type and number of animals they saw.

BROOKHOUSE FARM

They coloured their map and used a colour key to show where they saw each type of animal. They gave each field a letter.

The number in the middle of each field records the size of the field in acres.

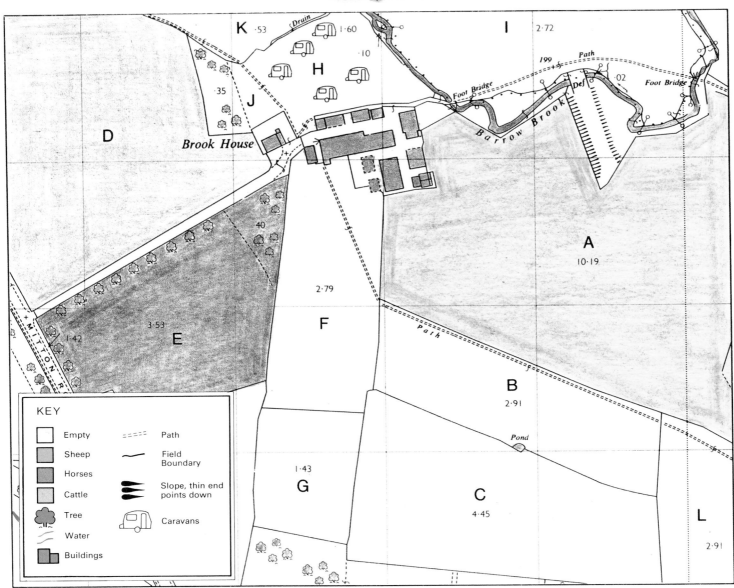

KEY

- Empty
- Sheep
- Horses
- Cattle
- Tree
- Water
- Buildings
- Path
- Field Boundary
- Slope, thin end points down
- Caravans

▶ List the fields in order of size.

Field	Acres
A	10.19
C	

▶ In which fields are the following animals kept? (a) sheep (b) horses (c) cattle

▶ Which fields are empty?

▶ Which animals can shelter under trees?

▶ Which two fields have a pond between them?

▶ As the children walk along the drive to the farm are the trees on their left or their right?

18

They drew a pictogram to record the number of animals they saw.

▶ Match the young to the adults.
e.g. a young horse is a foal

▶ How many (a) sheep (b) horses (c) hens did they see?

▶ How many young animals did they see altogether?

▶ Complete the sentences

The _____ lay eggs. The _____ are sold for beef. Wool comes from _____. The sheep are controlled by a _____. _____ hunt mice. _____ are kept for riding.

Animals around the farm

hens		11	cats		3
cattle		15	lambs		110
foals		1	chicks		14
sheep		80	kittens		2
dogs		4	horses		20
cock		1	calves		24

On their visit the pupils took these photographs.

▶ Match the photos with the map.

▶ In which fields were four of the photos taken?

▶ Where was the fifth photo taken?

Using Local Maps

Plan a visit to a nearby farm. Use the local 1:2500 Ordnance Survey Map.

▶ Make lists of the *similarities* (things that are the same as) and *differences* (things that are different from) Brookhouse Farm.

▶ If crops are grown find out the names of the crops and draw a pictogram. Ask when each is planted, harvested and what it is used for.

▶ Make a list of the buildings on the farm. What is each building used for?

Every year thousands of people enjoy visiting Safari Parks in Britain. To get the most from a visit you need to use a map of the Safari Park.

KNOWSLEY SAFARI PARK

▶ Begin your journey at the traffic signals. Use the chart to list in the correct order the animals you pass and on which side of the road you see them.

Animals	Left	Right
Guanaco		✓
Rhino	✓	
Bison		

▶ Where would these activities take place? Leave the car, Buy a gift, Eat a packed lunch, Play on a slide, Leave your dog, Buy a meal.

▶ Which is nearer to the pay boxes (a) the picnic area, or (b) the coach park?

▶ Which is nearest to the boating lake (a) the restaurant   (b) the kennels, or (c) Manager's office?

▶ Which is further from the elephant house (a) the amusement park, or (b) the kiosk?

▶ Which is furthest from the car park (a) the A58   (b) the traffic signals, or (c) the toilets?

▶ What might happen if you ignore the advice in (a) the 'Danger' box   (b) the 'litter' box? Write about and draw the possible results.

Animals at Knowsley come from all over the world.

 **Bi**
 **E**
 **La**
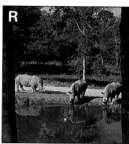 **R**
 **Z**

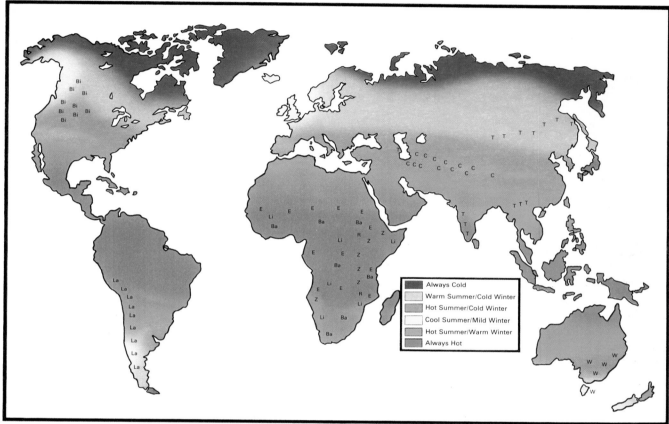

Always Cold
Warm Summer/Cold Winter
Hot Summer/Cold Winter
Cool Summer/Mild Winter
Hot Summer/Warm Winter
Always Hot

 **Ba**
 **Li**
 **T**
 **C**
 **W**

► Use information books and an atlas to help you complete the chart.

► Try and discover more about each animal.
What does it eat?
What does an adult weigh?
What are the young called?
How many young are born at the same time?

Photo	Name of Animal	Continent	Climates
Bi	Bison	North America	Warm Summer/Cold Winter Hot Summer/Cold Winter
E	Elephant		

Millions of people visit London every year.

To get the most out of a visit you need a map.

A map helps you decide where to go, how to get there and what to look for.

SIGHTSEEING IN LONDON

Look at the four photographs. They show some of London's famous tourist sites.

All four can be found on the map.

▶ In which grid squares is Buckingham Palace?

Name the roads that touch the palace gardens.

Which park is north of the Palace?

Which sport takes place there?

▶ Which road runs from Admiralty Arch to the Queen Victoria Memorial?

Which important building is it in front of?

What is the name of the lake to the east of the memorial?

▶ In which grid square is Nelson's Column?

Which road runs south from the Column?

Find out who Nelson was, when he lived and why he is famous.

In which famous square does Nelson's Column stand?

▶ In which grid square is Westminster Abbey?

Which famous building is east of the Abbey?

Which street passes in front of the Abbey?

Find out which King is buried behind the altar.

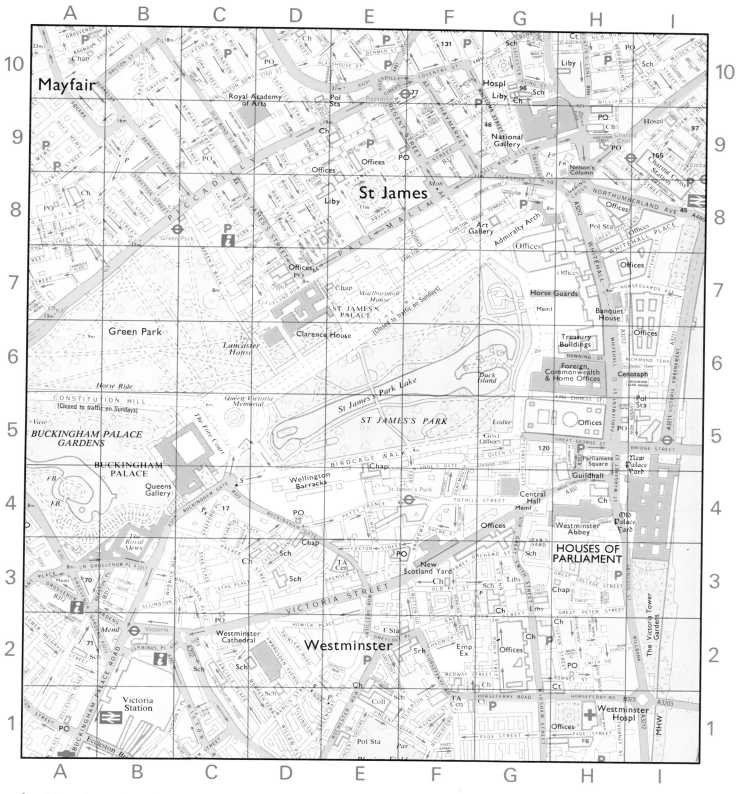

▶ Give the grid reference and say what happens at

(a) Houses of Parliament,
(b) Wellington Barracks,
(c) Clarence House,
(d) New Scotland Yard.

▶ Which roads would you travel along if you went —

From the Cenotaph to Charing Cross?
From New Scotland Yard to Victoria Station?
From Clarence House to the National Gallery?

▶ How many roads and sites can you find that are named after Kings or Queens?

Mr. and Mrs. Cole and their two children, Sam and Ruth, are on holiday with Mr. and Mrs. Peet and their daughter, Heather. They are visiting the Norfolk Broads for the first time.

HOLIDAY AFLOAT

This is a plan of the cruiser they have hired for the week.

▶ How many beds can you see?
▶ The seats in the galley are used as a double bed. Which other seats make a double bed at night?
▶ Copy and complete the chart for areas A to H.

	NAME OF AREA	ACTIVITY
A	Double Cabin	Sleeping, reading, relaxing
B		
C		

▶ Look at the plan and describe what each person is doing.
▶ Look at the photographs, name each area shown and say what is happening there.

▶ Look at the table plan, how many people are about to eat?
▶ Who do you think it will be?
▶ Make a list of what is on the table.

▶ Imagine your family had a holiday on this boat
▶ Where would each person sleep?
▶ Which jobs would each do?
▶ What would you most enjoy?
▶ Where would you spend most of your time?

The Peets and Coles could sail anywhere on the Norfolk Broads. They hired their boat at Wroxham and decided to sail to Great Yarmouth.

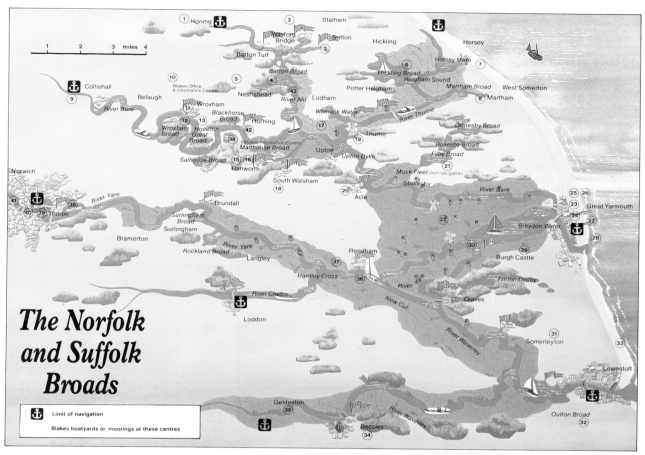

The Norfolk and Suffolk Broads

⚓ Limit of navigation

⚓ Blakes boatyards or moorings at these centres

PLACES TO VISIT — THINGS TO SEE AND DO

1 North Walsham & Dilham Canal (now abandoned)
2 Stalham Tuesday Market
3 Sutton Windmill and Pottery
4 Barton Nature Reserve
5 Beeston Hall
6 Hickling Nature Reserve and Water Trail
7 Windpump (preserved)
8 River green moorings, pubs and village
9 Horstead Millpool, lock (end of navigation)
10 Wroxham Barns Craft Centre
11 Roys — the largest village store in the world
12 Barton House Railway
13 Hoveton Great Broad Nature Trail
14 Cockshoot Nature Reserve
15 Ranworth Church — Cathedral of the Broads
16 Conservation Centre and Nature Trail
17 St. Benets Abbey (remains)
18 Fairhaven Garden Trust
19 Thurne White Mill
20 Acle Thursday and Sunday Markets
21 Thrigby Hall Wildlife Gardens
22 Stracey Arms Windpump (preserved)
23 Port of Yarmouth Marina
24 Municipal Yacht Station
25 Stadium — Greyhound racing/Stockcars
26 Racecourse
27 Marina Leisure Centre (pool and sports)
28 Pleasure Beach (permanent funfair)
29 Roman Fort (remains)
30 Berney Arms Windpump (preserved)
31 Somerleyton Hall (stately home and maze)
32 Nicholas Everitt Park and Yacht Station (Thursday evening powerboat racing)
33 Pleasurewood Hills American Theme Park
34 Municipal Yacht Station, Market town
35 Old Lock and inn
36 Broadland's only working Ferry
37 Pettitts Aviary, Feathercraft, Taxidermy
38 River Green
39 Norwich City Football Club
40 Yacht Station
41 Castle, Strangers Hall, and Bridewell Museums, Cathedral, Shopping, Theatre, Cinemas, Discos
42 Helska Leisure Centre and Horning Ferry Marina
43 How Hill Environmental Centre

▶ Which river would they sail on?
▶ Name the Broads they pass
▶ How many windmills will they pass on the journey?
▶ Why do you think it is impossible to sail past Coltishall?

Look at the 'Places to Visit' on the journey to Gt. Yarmouth.

Where could they —

▶ Stop to look at wild birds?
▶ Visit a ruined abbey?
▶ Shop at a market on Thursday?
▶ Ride on a roller coaster?

▶ Watch a greyhound race?
▶ Ride on a railway?

Which rivers join these towns?

▶ Norwich and Brundall
▶ Beccles and Somerleyton
▶ Loddon and Reedham

BY THE SEA

People visit the coast for different reasons. Some like steep cliffs for climbing or bird watching. Others enjoy playing and sun bathing on a sandy beach. When you decide which kind of coast to visit a map will help you choose a place that will suit you.

Look at the aerial photograph.

▶ Was it taken at high or low tide?
How do you know?
▶ What season was the photograph taken?
▶ What evidence tells you it was a nice day?
▶ What do you think the buildings facing the beach are used for?

Now use the map and photograph together.

▶ How many piers are there?
▶ Where is the lighthouse?
▶ Where are the boats moored?
▶ Why is it better to moor a boat in the harbour than on the other side of Smeaton's pier?
▶ Does the map show St. Ives at high tide or low tide?
▶ Draw a picture of the harbour at low tide on a sunny day.
▶ Draw the symbol used on the map for the church near the lifeboat station.
▶ Does this church have a tower or a spire?

▶ Look at the eight activities. Decide where each could take place. For some only one answer is correct, for others there is more than one possibility.

Copy and complete the chart. The first one is done for you.

Activity	Location	Grid Square
Sunbathing	Beach	

▶ Look at an O.S. map of a different coastline in Britain. What activities could you enjoy on a day visit there? How is it similar to and how is it different from St. Ives?

Princess Polly knows that only a kiss can wake Prince Percy. Use this picture to help you play the map game.

THE PRINCESS AND THE KEY

The first player to reach the castle will wake Prince Percy.
Throw a die and move in turn.
When you land on a purple space read the instructions shown
on the picture.

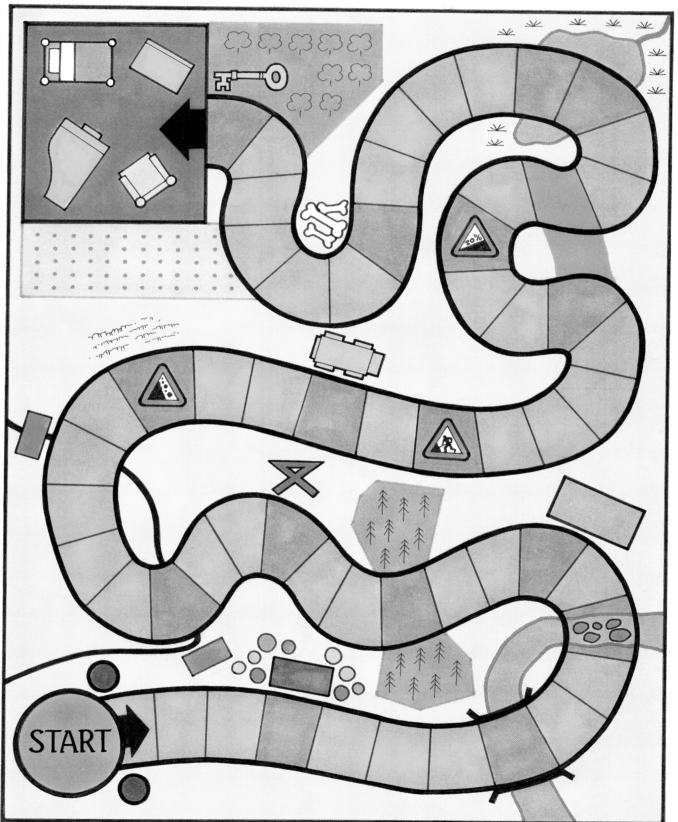

In order to put information on to maps the O.S. uses signs and symbols. Without them our maps would be covered with writing.

There are many different types of O.S. map. We choose a map which suits us best for the activity we are planning.

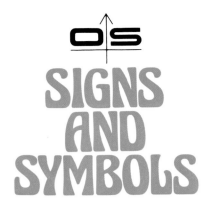

Different types of map use different signs and symbols. Each time we use a map we must look at the list of signs and symbols. Sometimes this is called 'signs' and sometimes 'legend'.

Signs and symbols from different O.S. maps have been drawn on this page.

ROADS AND PATHS

M 1	Motorway
A 1	Main road
B 676	Secondary road
– – – – –	Path

RAILWAYS

———————	Standard gauge track
—●—▬—	Stations

WATER FEATURES

	Lake
	Marsh
	Footbridge
	River
	Coniferous wood (Evergreen)
	Non-coniferous wood (Broadleaved)
	Orchard
☩	Church with tower
☗	Church with spire
+	Church without tower or spire

TOURIST INFORMATION

	Bus or coach station
⋏	Camp site
	Caravan site
▶	Golf course
𝒊	Information centre
P	Parking
✕	Picnic site
☎	Public telephone
	Skiing
	Viewpoint
	Wildlife park
P	Post office
P H	Public house
Sch	School
Castle	This kind of writing means the place is very old.

Look at the pictures which tell the story of two girls camping holiday.

▶ Write the story in your own words.
Use an O.S. symbol in the story whenever you can.
Here is an example of what you might do.

▶ Draw your own set of pictures based on nine other O.S. symbols. Ask a friend to write the story using words and symbols.

'Rita and Pam arrived at the ▭. They walked along the road until they reached the ⊠ where they put up their tent. Later they went for a walk between a ⬤ and a ▭ ---

Acknowledgements

Linda Edmondson
Head teacher and staff of Revoe School
Cannon F. H. Levick of Ribchester
London Tourist Authority
John and Dorothy Townson, Brookhouse Farm
Blakes Holidays
Knowsley Safari Park
Hoseasons Holidays
Scottish Tourist Board
Pontins
Aerofilms

Design by Barrie Richardson

Illustration by Barrie Richardson and David Wilson

Published in 1991 by
CollinsEducational
An imprint of HarperCollins*Publishers*
77–85 Fulham Palace Road
Hammersmith
London W6 8JB

Reprinted in 1992

First published 1988 by

Ordnance Survey and Holmes McDougall

Romsey Road   Allander House
Maybush   137/141 Leith Walk
Southampton   Edinburgh
SO9 4DH   EH6 8NS

Ordnance Survey ISBN 0 319 000 94X
CollinsEducational ISBN 0 00 316 139 0

Printed by Holmes McDougall Publishing and Print Limited